CONFORMATION

by

Pegotty Henriques

Illustrations by

Carole Vincer

THRESHOLD BOOKS

First published in Great Britain by
Threshold Books, The Kenilworth Press Limited
Addington, Buckingham, MK18 2JR

Typeset by DP Photosetting, Aylesbury, Bucks

Printed in Great Britain by Westway Offset

British Library Cataloguing in Publication Data

Henriques, Pegotty
    Conformation. – (Threshold picture guides)
    I. Title   II. Series
    636.12

    ISBN 187208222X

CONTENTS

Introduction

'Conformation' is the term used to describe the shape of the horse. Its skeleton and musculature are important, not merely for aesthetic value, but because good conformation enables the horse to be athletic and to stand up to hard work.

Few horses, if any, are perfect but an understanding of the basic principles of conformation will help the rider to choose a horse that is suitable for his own purpose.

The temperament and action are also important. There is no point in buying a beautiful horse if he is an unwilling worker, resentful or nappy.

To enjoy the pleasures of riding, training and competing, your horse should have:

- A willing attitude to his work.
- A friendly manner in his daily life.
- Good health and a sound constitution.

Without these attributes perfect conformation will be valueless.

You cannot change the skeletal structure or the natural talent of a horse but, as his muscles develop through work, his ability and appearance will alter.

Whilst the skeleton remains the foundation of the horse's conformation, the way he is muscled will tell you a lot about how he has been trained and ridden. As the muscles of a young, ungainly horse develop through correct training he often becomes more attractive.

When you first look at a horse it is important to study the whole picture. Nature can sometimes compensate for a fault; an asset can balance a defect.

The combination of the horse's physical and functional attributes makes him an ideal or valueless type.

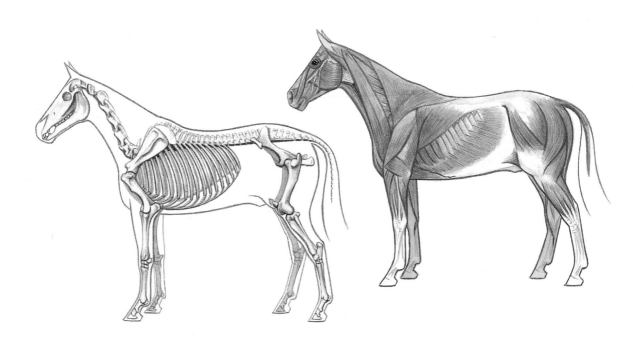

Proportion

Just as with humans, the horse should look proportionately right. It doesn't matter whether he is small or large – he should look in balance.

A well-balanced horse does not have an overweighted forehand. If his weight is distributed more towards the quarters he can carry a rider more easily. Because of the horse's structure, the rider tends to sit towards the front end, so the horse's natural balance is adversely affected.

A horse with a long neck and a big head will tend to have too much weight on his forehand. If his head is large but his neck is short, the weight of his big head will affect him less. Nature has compensated.

If a horse has a long neck that is set on in a low position he will again be weighted towards his forehand. A more highly set-on neck that is well carried has an advantageous effect on the horse's balance, provided that the neck is correctly muscled.

A short back is strong and often goes with powerful quarters. It can be uncomfortable to sit on. An over-long back is generally weak.

In a mature horse the height of the croup should be the same or lower than the withers.

A horse with comparatively short legs will lack athleticism. Long legs and a shallow rib cage may well indicate too little heart and lung space, essential for stamina.

A wide horse can be uncomfortable to sit on and tends to rock from side to side. A very narrow-chested horse may knock one leg against another.

Weak quarters and hind legs must be considered a serious defect.

A well-proportioned horse should fill the eye without drawing attention to any single attribute, good or bad.

Different types

There are many different breeds and types of horse and pony.

The **Thoroughbred** is fast, sensitive and intelligent. Bred to race, he can also be a brilliant jumper and a perfect riding horse. Generally comfortable and with good paces, he is quick to learn. Ridden and trained by a good rider he can be incomparable. Most modern sport-horses are partly Thoroughbred.

The **Arab** is renowned for his great stamina. His intelligence is great; his bones are fine but dense; his head is beautiful. He is not famed for his jumping ability. He is seldom big.

The best riding horse is often a cross-breed.

The **warmblood** has been bred as the ideal modern riding horse. He is a mixture of many breeds and bloodlines and was developed on the Continent through the crossing of indigenous stock with quality breeds: Thoroughbreds, Trakehners and Arabs. Warmbloods are generally named after their country or region of origin: e.g. Hanoverian, Westfalian, Swedish or Dutch Warmblood. They have achieved particular success in show jumping and dressage.

The **cob** is the result of cross-breeding. A true cob has the body of a horse on short legs and may not exceed 15.3 hh. He can be ridden or driven. Unlikely to have great speed, he is often a good jumper due to powerful hindquarters. He is tough and hardy.

The **draught horse** comprises many heavy breeds. The heaviest of all in Britain is the Shire, often standing over 17 hh and weighing a ton. Draught horses, although used principally for heavy farm work, were also ridden. Despite their massive size, strength and activity they are usually docile.

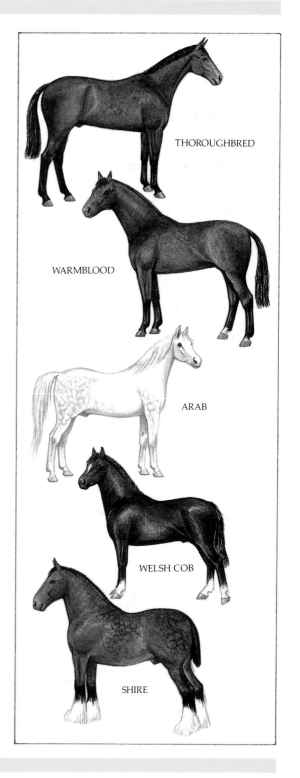

THOROUGHBRED

WARMBLOOD

ARAB

WELSH COB

SHIRE

The mind of the horse

The horse's temperament is expressed in his face. His eyes, ears, nostrils and head movements will tell you a great deal.

Large eyes, set well apart, denote intelligence and generosity. They should express interest, calmness and friendliness. The horse that will stand calmly whilst showing a keen interest in his surroundings can usually be relied on to have a good working temperament.

A dull eye combined with unpricked ears may well indicate a dreary ride or an unhealthy horse.

A horse with a very alert appearance and a lot of head movement might suit an experienced rider more than a novice.

Small eyes with a bump between them can indicate a stubborn streak. Some say that an eye surrounded by white is untrustworthy, but this theory is unproven.

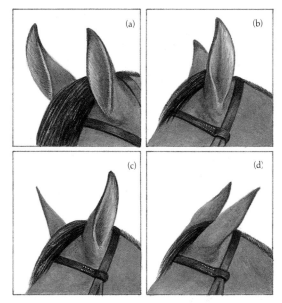

(a) Pricked ears look attractive but sometimes denote a lack of full attention to the rider. (b)–(c) These positions signify attention to the rider. (d) Confusion, distrust or bad temper.

DULL

ALERT AND CALM

HIGHLY SENSITIVE

PIGGY

SHOWING TOO MUCH WHITE

The head

Small, neat ears are considered attractive, but can accompany nervousness. Although not always appearing attractive, large ears are not a conformation fault and can enhance hearing. Bad hearing can cause nervousness.

The mouth should be examined carefully. The teeth should be correctly placed, the front teeth meeting and not overlapping as this will affect eating and digestion. The tongue groove should be wide enough to allow the tongue to lie comfortably and not be pushed upwards. The tongue should not be so fat that it bulges in the mouth and leaves insufficient room for the bit. If it does, there is little point in increasing its owner's discomfort by strapping his jaws together. Avoid such mouth problems. When a horse is uncomfortable in his mouth his good points are overridden and his character also affected.

Large, heavy lips and nostrils often denote commonness and insensitivity.

While the overall impression of the head and its expression are of great importance, so is the set and connection of the head and neck.

There should be plenty of space for at least two fingers directly behind the cheek bone, which should not be too large. A large bone combined with a thick neck frequently has a bulge of fatty tissue where the space should be. Obviously such a horse will find flexion uncomfortable, if not impossible. The point where the neck meets the head should be neither too thin nor too thick.

A big head adds weight to the forehand and is not attractive.

OPEN GULLET

Plenty of space for at least two fingers behind the cheek bone allows the horse to flex correctly.

HEAVY AT THE THROAT

Thickness at the throat and an abundance of fatty tissue make it hard for such a horse to flex. A large cheek bone adds to the problems.

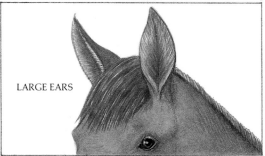

While neither small nor large ears are incorrect they should be in proportion to the head and express interest and attentiveness.

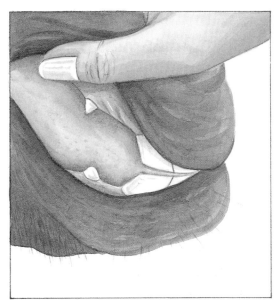

A large, heavy tongue leaves little room for the bit. This mouth is heavy lipped and could be insensitive.

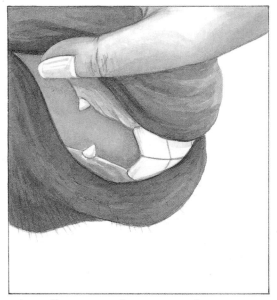

A small tongue and a neat mouth.

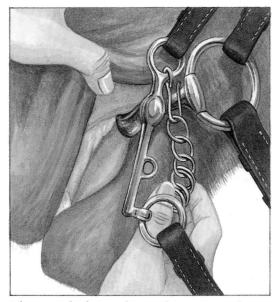

This mouth shows plenty of room, even for the double bit.

The topline

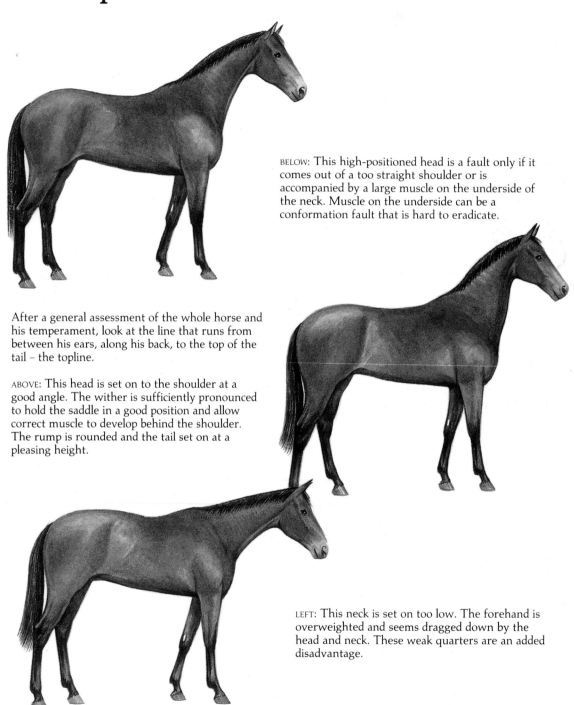

BELOW: This high-positioned head is a fault only if it comes out of a too straight shoulder or is accompanied by a large muscle on the underside of the neck. Muscle on the underside can be a conformation fault that is hard to eradicate.

After a general assessment of the whole horse and his temperament, look at the line that runs from between his ears, along his back, to the top of the tail – the topline.

ABOVE: This head is set on to the shoulder at a good angle. The wither is sufficiently pronounced to hold the saddle in a good position and allow correct muscle to develop behind the shoulder. The rump is rounded and the tail set on at a pleasing height.

LEFT: This neck is set on too low. The forehand is overweighted and seems dragged down by the head and neck. These weak quarters are an added disadvantage.

LEFT: The saddle sits too far forward on this horse because his wither is flat. His straight shoulder means that the rider is almost sitting on top of the forelegs, which would give a jarring uncomfortable ride and overload the horse's forehand.

RIGHT: This horse has a well-defined wither and a good sloping shoulder from wither to the point of the shoulder. The saddle sits much further back and the rider's weight will be in a better place for the horse's balance.

LEFT: The spine of this horse is high and straight. The saddle and the rider will be perched and the ride will be uncomfortable.

The topline (cont.)

During the horse's growing period his croup may appear higher than his withers. This usually evens out as he reaches maturity.

Ultimately it is desirable that the withers are higher than the croup. A high croup always gives the impression that a horse is on his forehand.

During his growing period a young horse will often appear croup-high. This is unimportant as long as his withers remain almost flat with his shoulders. But once the withers are well defined and prominent make sure that the croup is level or lower.

Excessive prominence of the withers without good muscling just behind the shoulders may lead to saddle-fitting problems. Check that a clear tunnel of light can be seen through the arch of the saddle when standing behind the horse.

A strong, supple back is an important asset. Only such a back will bring the hindquarters into an effective position of weight bearing, allowing the hind legs to step properly under the rider's weight and towards the horse's own centre of gravity.

Although young horses have not properly developed their loin muscles an indication of some muscling should be visible. There should be breadth of muscle under the back of the saddle to support the rider's weight. Check also that the area below the front of the saddle is not rounded or the saddle may slip to one side.

The spine behind the saddle should not be over-prominent. Once a horse is working effectively the loin muscles either side of the spine should be broad and raised.

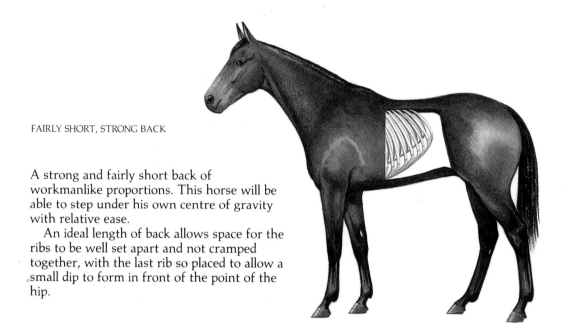

FAIRLY SHORT, STRONG BACK

A strong and fairly short back of workmanlike proportions. This horse will be able to step under his own centre of gravity with relative ease.

An ideal length of back allows space for the ribs to be well set apart and not cramped together, with the last rib so placed to allow a small dip to form in front of the point of the hip.

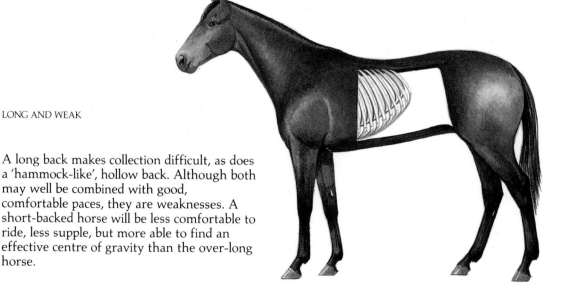

LONG AND WEAK

A long back makes collection difficult, as does a 'hammock-like', hollow back. Although both may well be combined with good, comfortable paces, they are weaknesses. A short-backed horse will be less comfortable to ride, less supple, but more able to find an effective centre of gravity than the over-long horse.

Behind the saddle

The energy which stems from the driving forces of the hind legs, must travel through the croup and back.

The shape of a horse's rump, combined with the angulation of the joints, can indicate his potential for speed, jumping or general athleticism.

Seen from the side, a fairly horizontal, wide, well-muscled rump with length from the point of the hip to the point of the buttock is considered good.

Viewed from behind, the points of the hips should be lower than the croup, forming a roof shape. The hips should be set well apart. A lack of speed and jumping ability stems from flatness across the croup to the point of the hips and is noted in the draught horse type. The greater the slope of the croup to the hips the more likely the horse is to jump well.

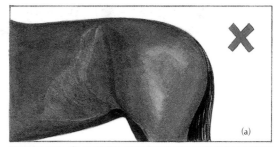

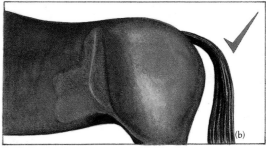

(a) A flat croup and weak muscular development. (b) A rounded rump, good distance to the point of the buttock and hip set lower than the rump.

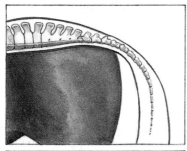

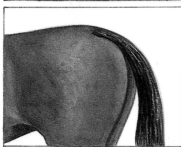

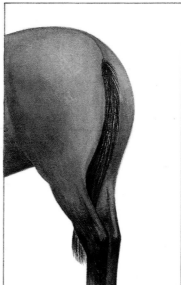

The tail is an important extension of the spine. Due to the corresponding angle of the joints, movement is impaired if it is set too high.

A horse that carries its tail clamped down fails to work through its back. A swinging tail signifies suppleness and energy.

The underside of the horse

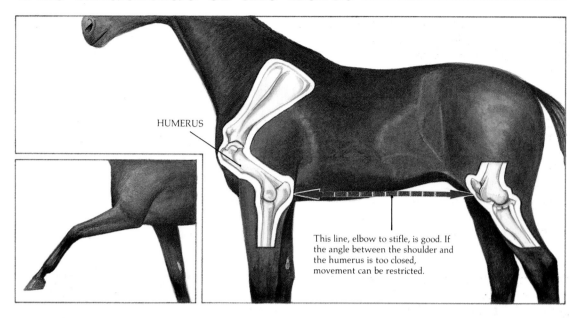

HUMERUS

This line, elbow to stifle, is good. If the angle between the shoulder and the humerus is too closed, movement can be restricted.

A big jaw bone, protruding into the neck, or heaviness through the throat, can hamper breathing and flexion. Thinness at the top of the neck gives similar problems. None of these faults encourages an easy head carriage.

The neck should flow smoothly into the chest, which should be clearly defined. The neck should be much deeper where it joins the shoulder than at the poll.

A big muscle under the neck, with only little muscle along the top, indicates a faultily set on head and neck or sustained bad training. A smooth, flowing underside muscle is desirable.

The stifle joint should not be markedly higher than the elbow, which puts a horse on his forehand. Nor should the belly line run directly uphill towards the stifle, as this can mean the saddle will slide backwards. A pendulous belly can be an indication of ill-health (windsucking) or a lack of fitness. It also goes with a hollow back.

If a horse's forelegs are too close together he will have a narrow chest and lack heart and lung space. If he is too wide at the chest his paces will be impaired and he will probably lack speed due to a tendency to rock.

A wide horse is uncomfortable as the widest part of his girth comes below a short-legged rider's knees, pushing the lower leg outwards.

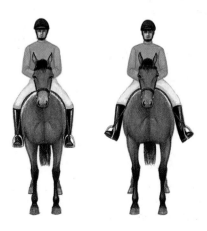

The shoulders and forelimbs

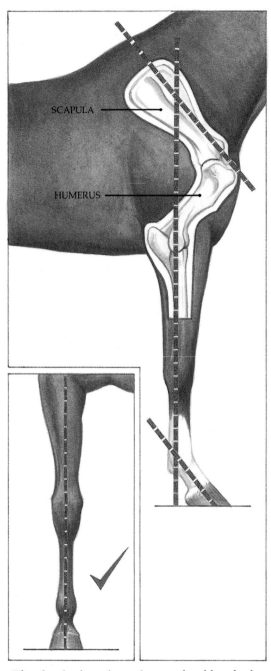

SCAPULA

HUMERUS

Ideally the shoulder should slope considerably forwards and should be flat and long. The raised central part of the shoulder blade (scapula) can be felt with the fingers and should run into the middle of the withers.

The angle of the humerus (from shoulder joint to elbow joint) should be fairly upright and not sloping severely backwards as this tips a horse forwards and impairs his movement.

The point of the elbow should not be too close to the horse but should offer enough space for a fist to be placed between it and the ribs. This ensures freedom of movement.

The measurement from the withers to the point of elbow should be roughly the same as from the point of elbow to the ground, and the ribs should not be flat but curved outwards. These attributes ensure lung and heart space.

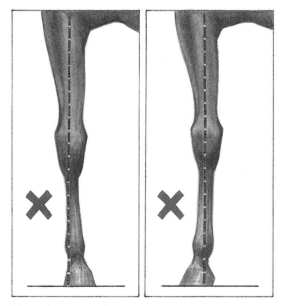

This forelimb with its sloping shoulder, fairly upright humerus and good length of muscled forearm can be equally appreciated from the front.

Straightness and symmetry are important. Avoid crooked forelimbs. They will put great strain on tendons, joints and ligaments.

Seen from the side and the front, the forelimbs should be straight and not slope backwards, forwards or be angled in or out.

The forearm should be long and the cannon bone short to give spacious movement.

The knee comprises a mass of bones but should appear flat and broad at the front with good depth.

Any variation from the symmetrical positioning of the limbs has to be considered a weakness.

Notable faults are:

- **Over at the knee**, when the horse seems to have his knee joint constantly bent forwards;
- **Back at the knee**, when the back of the knee seems pushed back and the front concave;
- **Tied in below the knee**, when the circumference of the bone is smaller than it is further down the cannon bone, which restricts the tendon;
- **Calf knees**, which are shallow from front to back and therefore lack strength.

The fetlock joints should be well defined and bony rather than rounded and puffy. Puffiness signifies strain and wear.

Short, upright pasterns will give a harsh ride while excessively long pasterns are weak and liable to strain.

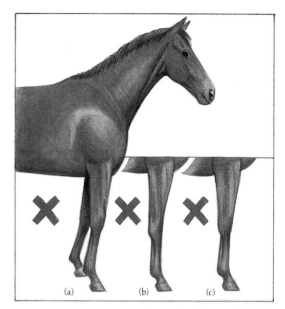

(a) **Over at the knee**, shows the joint looking bent. (b) **Back at the knee** looks concave at the front. (c) **Tied in** is narrow below the knee.

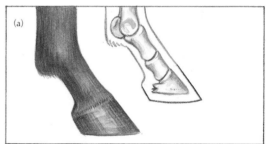

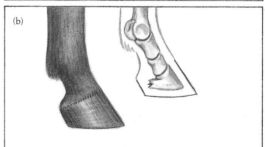

Well proportioned pasterns of reasonable length (a) add spring to the stride. Short pasterns (b) are likely to give a jarring ride.

The hind legs and hocks

As the horse advances in training more weight is placed on the hindquarters and correspondingly on the hocks and hind legs.

A horse with bad hindquarters and hind legs will therefore find advanced training difficult.

When a hind leg is well placed an imaginary vertical line should be traceable from the point of the buttock, down the back of the hock, continuing down the back of the hind leg to the fetlock.

The stifle joint should be close to the body but turned slightly outwards to allow free movement. If it is set out from the body the horse may have a wide action of the hind legs.

The hock is a very important joint. It should be wide when seen from the side and thick when seen from the rear. The overall appearance should be of bony strength.

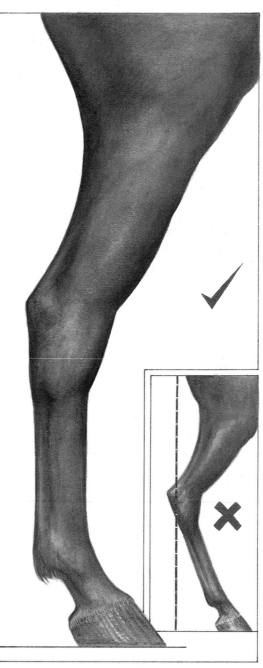

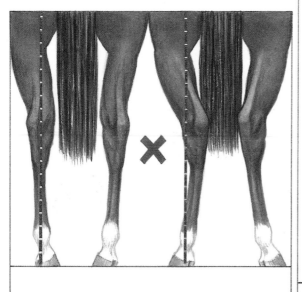

Turned-out hocks and hocks that point inwards (cow hocks) are both weaknesses that can cause malformation of the fetlock joints.

A good hind leg and hock (main picture). *Inset:* A sickle hock. This would be like sitting on a chair with a crooked leg!

Highly trained horses – through natural ability, training and exercises – develop great athletic ability. By learning to place their hind legs further under their bodies the overall distribution of weight is shifted, as much as possible, off the forehand. This makes it easier for them to stop, start, increase speed, turn sharply and jump while remaining in balance.

As a result of lighter weight on the forelimbs they suffer less wear and strain and the rider also enjoys far greater control and manoeuvrability. The power-house of the horse lies in his hindquarters. Great attention should be paid to their proportions and strength.

Feet

Good feet are essential and a subject on their own. More lameness comes from the feet than anywhere else.

Shape, quality and strength are the important attributes well detailed in *Threshold Picture Guide No. 16: Feet and Shoes.*

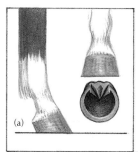 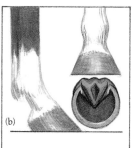

Boxy feet (a) have little bearing surface. The soles of **flat, spread feet** (b) have constant contact with the ground and suffer bruising.

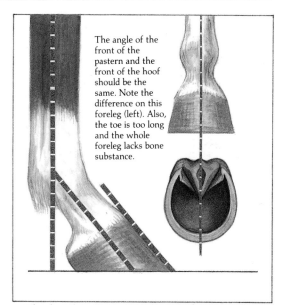

The angle of the front of the pastern and the front of the hoof should be the same. Note the difference on this foreleg (left). Also, the toe is too long and the whole foreleg lacks bone substance.

The height of the heel should be about half the height of the front of the foot. The foot should be symmetrical, with the forefoot circular and the heels well apart.

Musculature and condition

The basic shape of the horse is determined by his adult skeletal structure. It therefore has to be the most important attribute when determining conformation.

Muscles develop as the horse matures, adding beauty to his appearance and indicating how his development is proceeding.

Young untrained horses should give some indication of their muscle-developing tendencies.

Quality muscles are long and smooth and, through work, increase in size whilst maintaining the same qualities. Lumpy, thick, heavy muscles are not desirable in a riding horse and belong to the efforts of strength used by workhorses.

Fat acts as a disguise to both conformation and muscular faults. It is easier to judge the true conformation of a lean horse.

Particularly observe the topline neck muscles, those just in front of the withers (trapezius), the loin muscles and the flanks and thighs. Evidence should show their potential for development.

Be wary of incorrect muscular development such as uneven topline neck muscles, muscle under the neck and poor first and second thigh muscles.

When viewed from behind the muscles between the thighs should almost touch. If there is space and daylight, there is little muscle.

It is easy to confuse fat with muscle. Check how the ribs are covered. Extreme fat has a lumpy, solid texture.

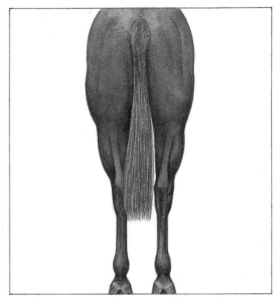

Well-muscled quarters give the appearance of the horse wearing trousers.

The smoothness of these neck and shoulder muscles is an indication of quality muscle and correct training.

Action

However beautiful a horse may appear when standing still, the way he moves must be satisfactory. Essential elements to observe are straightness, freedom and regularity.

See the horse led on a loose rein on a hard road; watch from the side, front and rear. The horse's legs should travel directly forward, on a straight line, the front feet remaining square throughout the stride and coming to the ground where the toe points.

The limbs should swing neither inwards nor outwards; the feet should not twist as they touch the ground.

There should be sufficient room for the fore and hind feet to pass each other without brushing. But if the legs are placed too far apart the horse may tend to lack athleticism.

The hind feet should follow directly behind the forefeet on the same side.

Although swinging a toe outwards (dishing) is considered a fault it can be due to a lack of strength and maturity. The fault, although aesthetically unattractive, is not necessarily severe unless the swing is initiated from the shoulder, when rocking becomes an additional problem.

Forelegs and hind legs should be watched to ensure that each pair takes a stride of equal length and height. Minute differences should be observed, particularly of height with regard to the hind legs, as this can be an early indication of spavins or stringhalt.

Freedom can be observed well in walk when the print of the forefoot is well overstepped by the hind foot. A free-moving horse has a looseness about his stride while remaining purposeful.

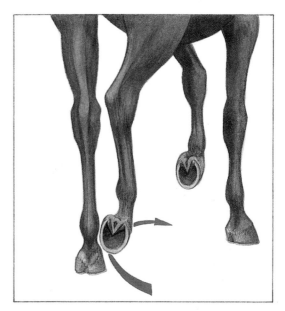

The hind legs here pass too close together and could cause continual damage through knocking against each other.

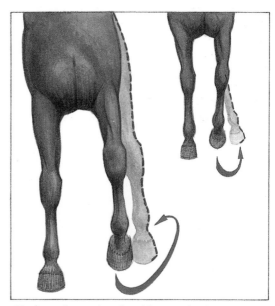

Dishing from the shoulder is a bad fault because it interferes with the balance of the horse. Merely 'turning a toe' is not so disadvantageous.

Paces

The horse should be observed in all paces, on circles to the left and right and on the straight.

Sometimes a relatively ugly horse will surprise you with the brilliance of his paces.

In walk there should be a marked and regular four beats to the stride and clear overtracking. Faults usually only observed when the horse is ridden include: the lateral walk, when the horse moves in two beats with the near fore and near hind travelling forwards at the same time followed by the off fore and off hind; and irregular beats instead of the clear 1-2-3-4.

In trot there should be a marked two beats to each stride, the diagonal pairs of legs moving forwards together and with a moment of suspension between each stride.

The essence of a good trot is spring and elasticity. The hind legs should be picked up and moved directly forwards and not left trailing out behind the horse.

In the past a low action was considered ideal, nowadays the modern horse is required to have a more rounded action.

The canter has a marked three beats with a short moment of suspension. The horse should spring into the air with each stride and not be stuck to the ground in a lifeless way.

In gallop a horse should cover as much ground as possible with each stride. Always try a horse in gallop for it is an indication of his heart and lung capacity as well as his overall ability.

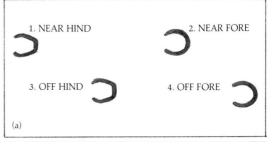

(a) The sequence of footfalls in walk. (b) The hind foot is seen to overtrack the print made by the forefoot.

Here the moment of suspension is pronounced and shows a very desirable degree of impulsion.

This canter has spring, life and balance. The horse moves forwards and upwards in his carriage.

This type of canter is often termed 'earthbound' because it lacks the impulsion that creates the moment of suspension. It is flat and dull to watch.

Jumping freely, this horse uses his head and neck without restraint. The well-folded front legs, bascule and technique are excellent.

By jumping too high, failing to fold his front legs, hollowing his back and raising his head, this horse clearly shows anxiety.

The ride

First watch the horse being ridden. Notice whether he is alert yet relaxed or lifeless and dull.

Take time to watch him thoroughly and see him in all paces, equally on both reins and over jumps. See how he re-settles once he has jumped.

Assess his natural balance. Does he seem athletic and find the work easy, or is he unco-ordinated?

In all paces his movements should go right through his body, and the joints of his limbs should be elastic and active.

Ride the horse yourself but never get on a horse that appears to be either unsuitable or dangerous.

In the saddle you should immediately feel comfortable – you should fit the horse just as your clothes fit you. If he is the right width your lower legs should be able to feel his sides without effort. This means that you will be able to apply leg aids correctly.

You should have the impression that you are sitting in the centre of a well-balanced machine. Obviously a very young horse will not give this sensation, but be cautious if he feels very ungainly.

Responsiveness and willingness should not be confused with nervousness. A horse should go forward willingly to your aids without being jumpy. He should not, however, be dull and lifeless. Try a tap with the stick. He should respond calmly.

All three paces should be comfortable.

Although many faults belong to bad training, be suspicious of a horse that has mouth and bitting problems.

A horse that really appeals to you, willingly accepts the bit, responds to the aids and stands still calmly may give you greater pleasure than a brilliant performer with a difficult temperament.

The first impression you have of a horse is often the right one. Never buy a horse that you do not instantly like. Never be persuaded to buy a horse that has given you a bad first impression. A horse's character is his most important attribute. If he has courage and willingness many conformation faults can be miraculously overcome.